# DIRTY

## DIRTY FOOD FOR YOUR FILTHY CHOPS

### MARK STUDLEY

# DIRTY

©2022 Mark Studley &
Meze Publishing Limited
First edition printed in 2022 in the UK
ISBN: 978-1-910863-90-9

Written by: Mark Studley
Edited by: Katie Fisher, Phil Turner
Photography by: Jean Philippe Baudey
at Faydit Photography
(www.fayditphotography.com)
Designed by: Paul Cocker
PR: Emma Toogood, Lizzy Capps
Contributors: Ekta Rajagopalan, Lis Ellis,
Lizzie Morton, Radha Joshi
Printed and bound in the UK by
Bell & Bain Ltd, Glasgow

@DirtyFoodGuy

me:ze PUBLISHING

FSC MIX Paper from responsible sources FSC® C007785

Published by Meze Publishing Limited
Unit 1b, 2 Kelham Square
Kelham Riverside
Sheffield S3 8SD
Web: www.mezepublishing.co.uk
Telephone: 0114 275 7709
Email: info@mezepublishing.co.uk

# CONTENTS

## FINGER GRABS

## NAUGHTY BURGERS

## DIRTY DOGS

# LOADED FRIES

# IN BREAD

# PHAAT PIES

# SAUCY STUFF

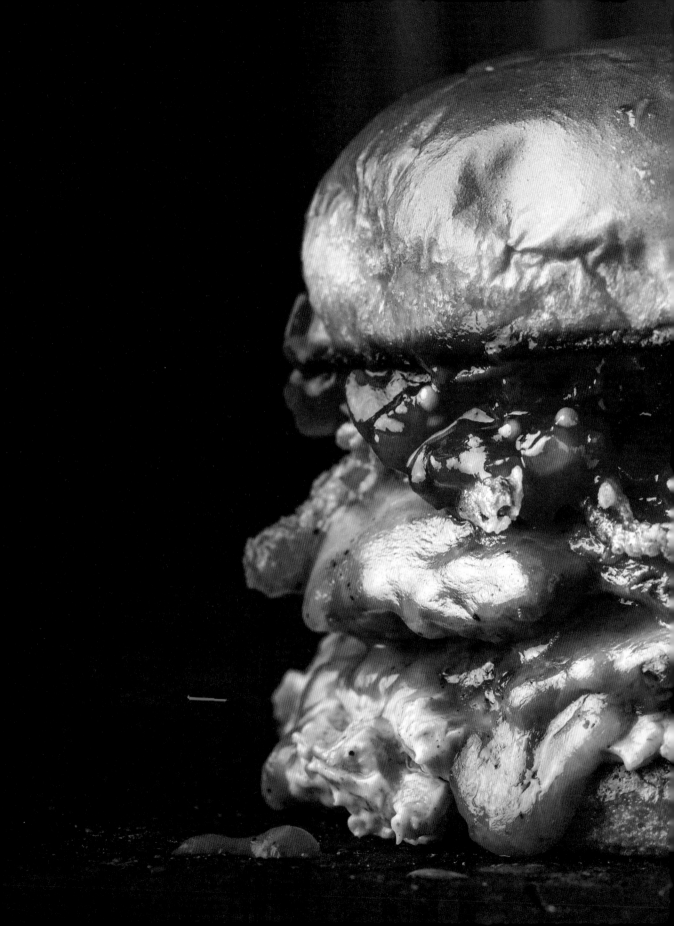

# INTRODUCTION

What is dirty food? It's food that gets your hands and face covered in deliciousness when you're eating it. It involves lots of sauce, lots of cheese and, in this book, lots of meat. Dirty food is about getting stuck in and not being shy to load up with a bit too much of the good stuff.

Dirty food is also a lot of what you see plastered all over social media these days. The never-ending bloggers, online critics, your mates, influencers... they're all eating it, and posting pics online that make you want to eat it too.

What you're about to read and learn in my recipes isn't faffy or fancy food; it's straight down the line, dirty, messy food. It's fun to make and, more to the point, fun to eat.

Although this is a cookbook, it's not the same as most other cookbooks in the sense that pretty much everything here is merely a base for you to build on and adjust to your own tastes. I'm not a Michelin-starred chef, or even professionally trained, and there are some things I'm really good at and some things I'm downright crap at.

But there's absolutely no shame in not being good at cooking, or feeling intimidated by recipes, or just loving jarred sauces and packets. I'm here to show you that making decent grub can actually be really easy, so easy that you'll amaze yourself and your family or mates and they'll never rib you about burning water again.

None of the recipes in this book are difficult, and there's nothing in here that should make you feel intimidated about attempting to cook it. There are no fancy ingredients, no big words, no fiddly methods, and no stupidly long times spent in the kitchen on a stupid number of processes to achieve a small end result. In fact, all the recipes in here are easily under an hour to knock up. Apart from just one ingredient in one of my recipes, you should be able to find everything you need at the local supermarket and crack on with making them.

All the recipes in this book can be adapted to your preferences, so please don't think you need to stick to my versions every time; this book isn't about that. Feel free to swap out the meats, change up the sauces or whatever you feel comfortable with. We all have our own individual tastes, and you might not like what I like, so I'm just giving you a guide to work from while showing you that all the great-looking dirty food you see online is easy to recreate and that you can have fun while doing it.

Unfortunately, if you're a veggie or vegan, this book won't be for you. While there are a few veggie options in here, I'm a meat eater, so this particular book involves meat, and lots of it. If loads of you buy this and it prompts me to do a follow up, I may do a load of dirty veggie food.

Just remember... It ain't good unless it's running down your chin.

# EQUIPMENT

This book is all about making food easy, so I use a few different pieces of equipment that you may or may not have, or even want to use for that matter. Ultimately, it's up to you how you do it but here's the main stuff I use.

Air Fryer – a great piece of kit that does what it says on the tin and does it well. Lots of different ones out there, but I'm using one of the Ninja ones that cost about £80... I think. My wife bought it and as usual I wasn't paying attention and to this day have no exact idea.

Pie Maker – clue's in the name. Awesome piece of kit as I'm not great at pastry making and when I make pies using a dish I always forget to put the baking ball things in and therefore cock it up. So, I invested in the Hairy Bikers pie maker, as it saves the stress and turns out great cooked pastry every time. Cost about £30. There are others out there that do the same job and are all a similar price.

Taco Holder – got them on Amazon and they're good for a couple of the recipes in here, although you'll want to use one for the actual cooking and then another for presenting. There are also some thick cardboard versions about, but you can't use those for cooking... obviously.

Cupcake/Muffin Tray – everyone has these, don't they? I use a deep one for some of the recipes in this book.

Saucepans – they're like me: everyone should have one (or two).

Deep-Sided Frying Pans/Woks – I use these to load up with oil for frying chicken etc.

Frying/Griddle Pans – you know what to do with these, right?

Baking Trays – for all the stuff we're gonna bake.

Squirty Bottles – if you're making your own sauces.

Let's get stuck in by coating our chops and fingers in awesomeness.

Coming up is food that's all about using your fingers, hands, or just face-planting and eating it like a dog... whatever you feel is appropriate at the time. I highly discourage using a knife and fork for eating these dishes because you don't want to be boring, do you?

Everything in this chapter is fun to make. Kids will love making some of it too and eating it, obviously. Much like the rest of the book that awaits you, finger grabs are about fun food for picking up, dipping, munching and generally enjoying getting sauce and whatever else over you.

Some stuff you might have seen before, some you won't have, and (as per the theme of this book) remember that my tastes might not be to your taste, so use these recipes as a base to start from. If you don't want to make any of the sauces and prefer to use a jarred sauce, go for it. Do it however you feel comfortable.

# FINGER GRABS

# BACON CHEESEBURGER WELLINGTON BOMBS

Turning your beef Wellington dreams into a crafty burger-flavoured version.

## YOU NEED

1 sheet of ready-rolled puff pastry

320g beef mince

80g mozzarella cheese

4 rashers of streaky bacon

1 tsp salt

⅛ tsp pepper

¼ tsp celery salt

¼ tsp garlic powder

Cooking spray or oil

2 slices of American burger cheese

1 pickle, diced

1 egg, beaten

Ketchup and mustard

## HOW YOU DO IT

Get the oven on and heated up to around 220°c. Get your puff pastry out the fridge and let it get to room temp as per the packet instructions.

Split the mince into 4 equal balls and then flatten them out. Cut the mozzarella into 4 chunks and stick one in the middle of each mince patty, then shape the patties into balls around the cheese, making sure the cheese is totally covered and not coming through. Wrap a bacon rasher around each ball and secure it with a cocktail stick. Mix the salt, pepper, celery salt and garlic powder in a bowl.

Get a frying pan on a medium heat and spray a bit of oil in, then add the stuffed and wrapped meatballs to sear the bacon all over. Sprinkle them with your seasoning mix, then turn and season again but be careful not to overdo it. You don't need to cook the meatballs themselves at this stage, just make sure they've had a blast of heat all over, by which point the bacon should have cooked and sealed so you can remove the cocktail sticks.

Cut the pastry into quarters big enough to fully cover the balls. Divide the American cheese and diced pickle evenly between the squares, then put the meatballs in the middle and fold them up.

Put the Wellington bombs on a baking tray lined with greaseproof paper. Brush the egg wash all over the pastry, including underneath, and then slam in the hot oven for about 25 minutes or until the pastry is a nice golden colour all over. If you want, turn the balls on their sides and pop back in the oven for 5 minutes to make sure the bottom is crispy as well.

Take out and dip in ketchup, mustard, or whatever you want.

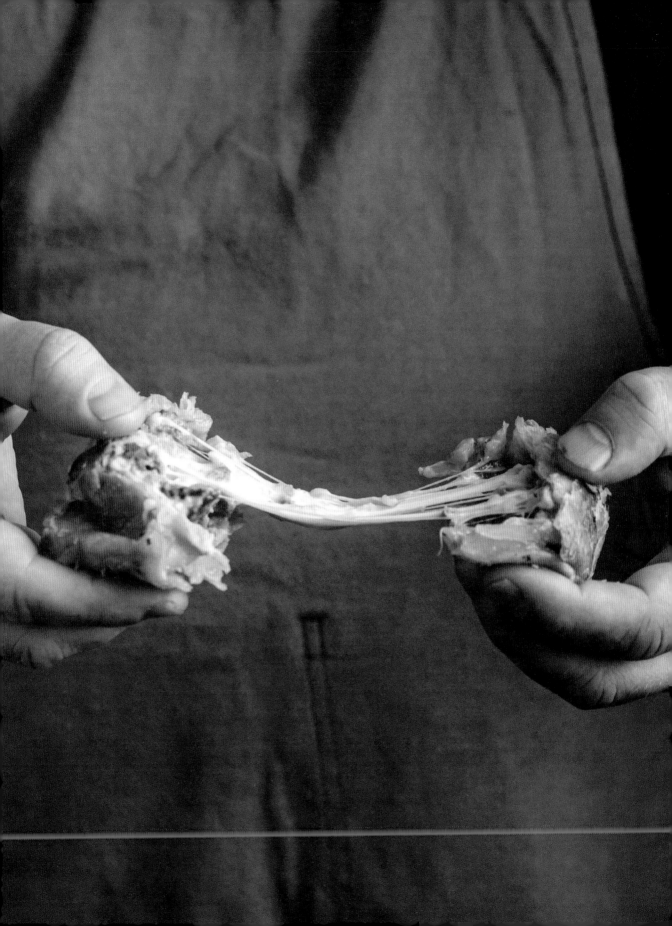

# BEEF WELLINGTON TACOS

Puff pastry taco shells are all the rage, didn't you know? Well...
they're not, but you just might play your part in making them all
the rage with this recipe.

## YOU NEED

1 sheet of ready-rolled puff
pastry

1 egg, beaten

4 big handfuls of spinach

8-10 slices of pancetta

1 big steak or 2 smaller ones
(ideally a nice thick ribeye,
sirloin or fillet)

Salt n pepper

1 heaped tbsp butter

2 cloves of garlic, peeled

2 sprigs of fresh thyme

4 heaped tbsp mayo

1⅛ tbsp wholegrain mustard

## HOW YOU DO IT

Get the oven on at about 200-220°c. Put a bowl (breakfast bowl
sort of size) upside down on the sheet of pastry and cut round
it to make a circle, then repeat so you have 2 cut outs. Line a
baking tray with greaseproof paper and put the pastry circles
on it. Brush the beaten egg over the pastry and put the tray in
the hot oven.

When one side of the pastry is nice and golden, flip it over and
let the other side cook for a couple minutes. I find that pressing
down on the pastry now and again to stop it really puffing up
during cooking helps to get the right shape afterwards.

When pastry is cooked, balance a wooden spoon between 2 upside-
down pint glasses and then drape the pastry over the handle of
the spoon with the least cooked side facing down. Gently bend
the pastry around the spoon and then leave for a couple minutes
to set.

Put the spinach in a deep bowl, add enough boiling water to cover
it and put a plate over the top to keep the heat and steam in
until you need it in a bit.

In the meantime, cook the pancetta in a frying pan on a medium-
high heat until nice and crisp (a few minutes all in) and then
set aside. Using the same pan, get it nice and hot before adding
the steak. Season with salt n pepper, then add the butter, garlic
and thyme to the pan. Baste the meat with the melted butter
and rub the garlic and thyme on the steak. When the steaks are
cooked to your liking, take them out the pan and let them rest
for a few minutes.

In a small bowl, combine the mayo and mustard while the steaks
rest. Mix well. Drain the spinach and squeeze out any excess
water, then cut the steaks into nice slices.

Ready to build these suckers? Let's go from the bottom up: your
puff pastry taco shells; a load of spinach; some crispy pancetta;
nice slices of steak; then a dollop of mustard mayo.

# CHEESEBURGER ROLY POLY

Here's a savoury version of the legendary Jam Roly Poly that we've all had at some point in our youths. In theory, this is probably the hardest thing to make in the book, but it's actually pretty straightforward and easy so let's get it out the way now.

## YOU NEED

4 good-sized spuds

2 eggs

Handful of grated cheddar

2 tbsp finely chopped fresh parsley

$\frac{1}{2}$ - $\frac{3}{4}$ tsp salt

$\frac{1}{4}$ - $\frac{1}{2}$ tsp ground black pepper

3-4 rashers of streaky bacon, diced

$\frac{1}{2}$ onion, diced

500g beef mince (approx.)

Squirt of ketchup

Squirt of mustard

1 pickle, finely chopped

200-250ml boiling water

Handful of grated mozzarella

Handful of grated Red Leicester

## HOW YOU DO IT

Get the oven preheated to 180ºc. Meanwhile, peel the spuds and then grate them into a bowl. Grab handfuls of the potato and squeeze the water out, then transfer to a dry bowl.

Add the eggs, grated cheddar, chopped fresh parsley, salt and pepper to the grated and drained spuds and mix it all together well.

Grab a baking tray and line it with greaseproof paper, then empty the contents of the bowl onto the tray and spread out evenly to cover it. Make sure there are no holes or gaps in the mixture (this is essential). When you're happy with that, lob it in the hot oven for 20 minutes.

In the meantime, cook the diced bacon and onion in a frying pan. Add the mince and cook until browned, then stir in a good squeeze of ketchup and mustard along with the pickle.

Pour the boiling water into the mince mixture, mix everything together well and then leave the pan on the heat for a couple more minutes until the water has been absorbed.

Bring the baked potato layer out of the oven and spread the meat mixture on top, covering the whole surface. Sprinkle a good load of the remaining cheeses all over it.

At one end of the tray, grab the greaseproof paper and use it to roll up the topped potato right to the other end. Make sure the roll is nice and tight, and obviously move the greaseproof paper out the way during the process.

Slide the roly poly off the paper completely and position it on the tray with the join underneath, so it can seal up as it finishes cooking.

Sprinkle some more cheese over the top and then bang the roly poly back in the oven for another 15-20 minutes. When done, cut into slices as thick as you want and serve hot.

# CHICKEN GYRO TWIRLS

A bit like them iced things in the bakery, only with meat and cheese and sauce... so loads better.

## YOU NEED

4 tbsp mayo

⅛ lime, juiced

½ tbsp honey

400g chicken strips

1 tsp Cajun seasoning

1 tsp garlic powder

1 tsp salt

1 tsp ground black pepper

1 sheet of ready-rolled puff pastry

1 egg, beaten

9 slices of burger cheese

Grated mozzarella

Bloody Mary ketchup to serve (see page 138)

## HOW YOU DO IT

Whack the oven on to about 200-210°c. Grab a flat baking tray and line it with greaseproof paper. Mix the mayo, lime juice and honey together in a small bowl. Add seasoning or more flavourings as needed to suit your tastes.

Dice the chicken up into small bits (a bit bigger than mince but not full-blown chunks) and put in a bowl. Throw the Cajun seasoning, garlic powder, salt and pepper onto the chicken and mix it all up so the meat is fully coated.

Get a pan and fry the chicken on a medium heat. Once done, put it to one side in a bowl. Cut the puff pastry into 6 equal strips lengthways. Grab the beaten egg and brush it around the edges of the first strip. Tear the burger cheese into strips and lay some down the middle of the puff pastry strip. Spread the honey-lime mayo over the cheese, then sprinkle the chicken on top, leaving a gap of about 1cm at each end. Sprinkle some grated mozzarella over the meat and then start to roll it all up from the near to the far end.

Lay the twirl flat side down on the lined baking tray and repeat with the remaining strips of pastry. When they're all done, brush the rest of the beaten egg over all the pastry (top and sides) and then cook in the hot oven for about 20-25 minutes, or until the pastry is cooked and a nice golden colour.

When ready, bring them out the oven and rest for a couple minutes to cool slightly. Plate up and serve with Bloody Mary ketchup or more of the mayo.

# CROQUE MONSIEUR BONBONS

Have some fun with mash, or even use Smash if you're proper lazy and can't be arsed cooking up some spuds.

## YOU NEED

### FOR THE MASH

5-6 medium spuds

Knob of butter

Pinch of ground black pepper

Good handful of grated red cheese

Good handful of grated mozzarella (use more for the ultimate cheese pull)

Small handful of grated cheddar

Couple slices of good ham, finely chopped

1-2 tbsp finely chopped parsley

### FOR THE COATING

3 tbsp plain flour

1½ tbsp cornflour

1½ tsp garlic powder, plus a pinch

1½ tsp salt n pepper, plus a pinch

1 large egg

5 tbsp golden breadcrumbs

2 tbsp grated hard cheese

Oil for shallow frying

## HOW YOU DO IT

Peel the spuds and cut them into small cubes, then chuck into a saucepan of water and bring to the boil. Meanwhile, prep your ingredients for the coating. Put the plain flour and cornflour in a bowl and add a pinch of garlic powder, salt and pepper. Crack the egg into another bowl and beat. Get a plate and put the breadcrumbs on it, then add the hard cheese, garlic powder, salt n pepper and mix it all up really well.

When the spuds are cooked, drain them, add the butter and then mash them up until smooth. Add the black pepper, cheeses, ham and parsley. Mix together well.

Grab a plate or tray and line it with greaseproof paper. Spoon out some of the mash mix and shape it into balls (about the size of a golf ball) and put them on the greaseproof paper. Do this until all the mash is formed into little balls. Stick them in the fridge for at least 1.5-2 hours, or until fully chilled and firm (if not chilled enough, they'll break when frying which you don't want).

Get a deep-sided pan with at least 1.5-2 inches of oil in (or a deep fat fryer) on a medium-high heat. Roll the mash balls in the flour coating, making sure they're covered all over, then do the same in the beaten egg and the breadcrumb mix until fully coated.

Put the bonbons in the hot oil to cook in batches, turning occasionally so they don't burn and the coating is crispy all over. When cooked, take out and drain the oil off.

Once all the bonbons are done, put them into a big bowl or plate, sprinkle some salt and grated hard cheese over the top and serve with dips of your choosing.

# MEATBALL PIZZA TACOS

Just because. Stop asking questions and get stuck in.

## YOU NEED

400g beef mince

⅛ tsp dried mixed herbs

⅛ tsp garlic powder

⅛ tsp black pepper

¼ tsp salt

1 ball of mozzarella

Oil or cooking spray

1 tin of chopped tomatoes

½ tbsp tomato purée

2 mini cheese pizzas

Taco tray for cooking on

Good handful of grated mozzarella

Dried oregano to taste

## HOW YOU DO IT

To make the meatballs, put the mince in a bowl with the mixed herbs, garlic powder, black pepper and salt. Mix in the seasoning with your hands, then divide the mince evenly into balls. Chop the ball of mozzarella into as many chunks as you have meatballs, about 1cm each. Get a ball and flatten it out, then put a chunk of mozza in the centre. Wrap the meat around it and shape back into a ball. Repeat with the rest.

Put the meatballs in a hot pan with a bit of oil and sear them off, then add the tinned toms and purée. Mix it all up to coat the meatballs. Simmer for 10-15 minutes, stirring occasionally and turning the balls over to ensure they're cooking evenly.

Meanwhile, heat the oven to around 200-220°c. When hot, cook the mini pizzas on the taco tray and take them out when almost done.

Spoon 3 meatballs into each pizza taco shell, cover with the sauce and then sprinkle over the grated cheese and oregano. Put the pizza tacos back in the oven for 7-8 minutes to let the cheese melt and the meatballs finish cooking through. When done, pull the tray out and fill your faces.

# PACHOS (INDIAN NACHOS)

These are slightly different to nachos, in the sense that they're made from broken up poppadoms instead of tortilla chips, and they're a right treat. You can fry the poppadoms yourself or use pre-made ones for an even quicker result.

## YOU NEED

I curry of your choice (see page 126)

I portion of pilau rice (homemade or from a packet is fine)

2 small onion bhajis

4 or more poppadoms

Pickled chillies, sliced

Garlic chilli mayo

Mango chutney

Raita

## HOW YOU DO IT

Get your curry, rice and bhajis made or reheated, and your sauces if you've not bought them. If you're making your own pickled chillies, they'll need doing a day or so ahead.

If frying your own poppadoms, pour about 2.5cm of vegetable oil into a deep pan over a medium heat. If you've already made your own bhajis, use the same oil. Either fry the poppadoms whole or break them into nacho-sized pieces first. Cook in batches and drain on kitchen roll.

Build your 'pachos' from the bottom up like this: some poppadom pieces; a sprinkle of rice; a few chunks of bhaji; sliced pickled chilli to taste; a bit of each sauce; and some curry.

Repeat the layers until you've used everything up, then top with a good dollop of each sauce and get stuck in. This makes a good-size bowl for 2 to share. Want it bigger? Double the stuff needed and go all out.

# PIZZA HASSELBACKS

Potato + pizza, all in one little bundle of joy.

## YOU NEED

10-12 small potatoes (not baby ones but not ya normal size either)

2 chopsticks or 2 knives of the same size

Sliced pepperoni (or any meat you want)

25ml olive oil

2 tbsp grated hard cheese (like parmesan)

Couple handfuls of grated mozzarella

Dried oregano to taste

## FOR THE GARLIC BUTTER

3 heaped tbsp butter

$1\frac{1}{2}$ - 2 tbsp garlic powder

1 tbsp dried mixed herbs

## FOR THE PIZZA SAUCE

100ml passata

1 tsp garlic powder

$\frac{1}{2}$ tsp mixed herbs

$\frac{1}{2}$ tsp each salt n pepper

## HOW YOU DO IT

First, get the oven warmed up to 220°c. Wash the spuds and pat dry. One at a time, put a spud between the chopsticks or knives and then start to cut slices about a couple mm thick – it's up to you exactly how thick you want them – down to the chopsticks or knives, so they stop you going all the way through. When the spuds are done, put them sliced side up in a roasting tin.

Insert a slice of pepperoni (or your choice of pizza meat) into each cut on the spuds. Cut the pepperoni to size where needed to help it fit. Brush the olive oil over the spuds and then put them in the hot oven for about 25 minutes.

Meanwhile, make the garlic butter by mixing the ingredients together. Use all the garlic powder if you want a stronger flavour. Next, make the pizza sauce by mixing all the ingredients together fast to blend well. Add more flavourings to suit your own tastes if you want.

When cooked, take the Hasselback spuds out the oven but leave them in the tin. Brush the garlic butter over the spuds, then spoon the pizza sauce onto each one. Add a sprinkle of the grated hard cheese, then the grated mozzarella and finally a sprinkle of oregano.

Put the Hasselbacks back into the oven until the cheese is all melted. To serve, put them in a bowl or on a plate and help yourself.

# SPAG BOL 'CUPCAKES'

A different take on an old British classic... sorry, I mean Italian. Just pick 'em up and eat 'em like a cupcake.

## YOU NEED

200g spaghetti

5 tbsp tinned chopped tomatoes

3 tsp dried mixed herbs

I tsp garlic powder

⅛ tsp each salt n pepper

50g grated cheddar

20g mozzarella

½ onion, finely diced

150g beef mince

Glug of red wine

½ tbsp tomato purée

I tin of chopped tomatoes

2 cloves of garlic, crushed

2 tbsp grated parmesan

Cooking spray

Cupcake or muffin tray

## HOW YOU DO IT

Preheat the oven to 180-200°c. Get a saucepan of water boiling and then drop the spaghetti in to cook. Mix the 5 tablespoons of chopped tomatoes with I teaspoon of the mixed herbs, the garlic powder, salt and pepper in a frying pan over a medium heat.

When the spaghetti is done, drain and add it to the pan of sauce. Stir to coat the pasta for a couple of minutes, then take off the heat.

Get the muffin tray and coat with cooking spray all around each section. Put a good spoonful of grated cheddar into each section, spreading it over the bottom and up the sides.

Get a long utensil like a fork or tongs in the spaghetti and twist to get a portion of the right size for the muffin tray. Plonk it on top of the cheese and repeat to use up all the saucy spaghetti.

Roll the mozzarella into balls about the size of a penny, then put one into the middle of each spag cupcake and push it about halfway down. Put the muffin tray in the hot oven for 25 minutes.

In the meantime, while the spag is in the oven doing its thing, get a pan hot and then add the onion. Cook until soft, stir in the beef mince and continue cooking until the meat has browned. Add the wine and simmer until it reduces slightly, then stir in the tomato purée, chopped tomatoes, garlic and the rest of the mixed herbs. Add a pinch of salt and pepper to taste, or other seasoning to your liking. Leave to simmer so the sauce reduces considerably.

When the spaghetti cupcakes are done, take the tray out the oven and leave for 2 minutes to make sure they set in place. Carefully extract each one; they should have a nice cheese crust around the base and part of the sides and the spaghetti will be set in the shape of a cupcake and not fall apart when lifted. If they do fall apart, they need to go back in the oven for a bit longer.

Put the cupcakes on a plate, spoon the meat sauce on top of each one and sprinkle with the grated parmesan, then pick them up and eat with your hands. If you want to jazz them up, drizzle some garlic mayo or another sauce over the top.

# AUGHTY
# URGERS

Burgers are a big deal these days. There are so many burger joints, burger stalls, burger books, burger people, burger critics, burger bloggers... it's unreal. It's probably because the possibilities with burgers are endless and there's so much you can do with them, but there are also a few components to a burger that you need to get right. To me, the key parts of a great burger are:

The Buns. You want a bun that can hold the glorious mess you're making and eating, so you don't want it to crumble at the first hurdle. The good ones in the supermarkets tend to be brioche but there are a few others out there to choose from. The bun should always be toasted prior to you loading it up.

Meat. Ideally, you want a good blend of say chuck and brisket, from a good butcher. I know not everyone has access to or money for that, but you can still make stuff that's equally good from the supermarket meat counter. As long as it has at least 15% fat, you'll be onto a winner, as the fat is what gives the meat a good dose of flavour. Never season the meat when mixing it up, and never add egg, breadcrumbs or anything else. You just want the meat. Adding salt to the meat and then mixing it up will cause the beef to start breaking down and you'll get that very cheap sausage meat texture when you're biting into it.

Cheese. You can use good old plastic burger cheese, or grab yourself some sliced red Leicester, smoked applewood, Mexicana, Monterey Jack... there are so many options to choose from. I have my faves and that's what I'll be using in this section, but again, you can change it up to use whatever you want. It's all about your own tastes, not mine.

Sauce. No burger is complete without the right sauciness. It's got to be the right combination to get the full flavour effect.

Seasoning. I tend to use salt n pepper, mixed with a bit of garlic powder and celery salt (say 3 tbsp salt, 2 tbsp ground black pepper, ¼ tbsp celery salt and ¼ tbsp garlic powder). Or just plain old salt n pepper together, about a 50/50 blend.

There are also a few different ways to cook burgers at home. In general, you only want to flip them once and never push down on them while cooking. You want them to be juicy, not dry and crispy. Throughout the recipes in this section, I just say "choose your cooking method" and then you need to cook the burger as outlined below. Here are the three main approaches:

Standard (120g to 140g). Shape the meat into a burger and then fry it until done to your liking. You ideally want to double or triple these patties when assembling your burgers.

Smash (110g to 140g). Form the meat into a ball, then get the frying pan very hot and put the ball into the pan. Leave it for a minute or so, then put some greaseproof paper on top of the ball and use a flat utensil to push down and flatten out to the desired thickness. Remove the paper and let it form a nice crust on the first side, making sure you season it, before flipping it over to season again and cook on the other side until done to your liking. Again, these are ideal for doubling or tripling up in your burger buns.

Pan to Oven (180g to 220g). This is my go-to method when I want to make a nice chunky burger. Preheat your oven to about 220°c. Shape the burger using your hands. Get a frying pan nice and hot, then put the burger in the pan and season the top side. Cook for a couple of minutes, then flip it over, season and leave for a couple more minutes. Remove from the heat, transfer the burger to a baking tray and put it in the hot oven to finish cooking for about 8-10 minutes, depending on how you want it cooked and how thick the burger is. Finish off by placing a cheese slice on top of the burger to melt in the oven. I'd only use one of these patties in a bun, but you can double up if you want full on meat sweats.

# BELLY BURGER

Belly's gonna get ya with this loaded-up treat.

## YOU NEED

1 belly pork strip

1⅛ tbsp BBQ sauce

1⅛ tbsp runny honey

1 burger bun

1 heaped tbsp chimichurri mayo (see page 141)

1 heaped tbsp Bloody Mary ketchup (see page 138)

1 burger patty (see page 43)

1 slice of American burger cheese (or whatever cheese you want to use)

1 medium-size chilli, thinly sliced

1 tbsp crispy onions (homemade or from a tub)

⅛ tbsp finely chopped fresh chives

## HOW YOU DO IT

Preheat the oven to 200°c. Put the belly pork into a roasting tin and whack it in the oven. After 25 minutes, turn it over. After about 45 minutes, mix the BBQ sauce and honey in a bowl and then spoon this over the belly pork, turning it over to coat on both sides. Put it back in the oven for about 20-25 minutes, turning one more time halfway through. When belly is nice and tender like butter, take it out the oven and leave to rest.

Meanwhile, grease a frying pan with oil or cooking spray and toast the bun cut sides down. Spread the chimichurri mayo on the base of the bun and the Bloody Mary ketchup on the top half.

Make up and cook the burger patty according to your method of choice (see page 43) and put the cheese on top. Top with sliced chilli to taste. Lay the cooked belly pork on top and steam the lot so the cheese melts. You can do this in a hot frying pan with a tiny bit of water splashed in and the lid on, or a hot oven. Sprinkle on the crispy onions and chives, then finish with the top bun and get stuck in.

# CHILLI BEEF

A little bit of hot, a little bit of sweet, this beaut has it all.

## YOU NEED

2-3 tbsp baconnaise (see page 138)

I tsp chipotle chilli flakes

I burger bun

I onion

I good-sized chilli, sliced

2 beef burger patties (or I thick one – see page 43)

2 slices of Mexicana cheese

Chilli jam

## HOW YOU DO IT

First, make the sauce. Stir the baconnaise and chilli flakes together until everything is mixed well. Add more sauce, seasoning or whatever you want to get the taste right for you.

Reheat the pan you used to cook the bacon for the baconnaise and toast your bun cut side down in the fat, giving it a nice golden brown colour. When done to your liking, set aside but keep the pan hot.

Halve the onion and then cut a slice from the widest part about 2mm thick. Put this into the hot pan and let it cook, flipping occasionally but being careful not to break the slice up so it stays whole. Cook until the onion is soft and has a tasty char on it. Cook the sliced chilli at the same time as the onion, turning occasionally, until it's nicely charred (but not burnt).

Make up the burger patties and get them boys cooking according to your method of choice (see page 43). When they're nearly ready, lay the cheese slices on top and get them melted.

Now build your burger from the bottom up like this: bottom bun, chipotle baconnaise, the first cheese-topped patty, some sliced chilli (let it melt into the hot cheese), the second patty, the charred onion and then the top bun, spread thickly on the toasted side with chilli jam.

Dirty in the sense that it gets your mouth and face filthy.

## YOU NEED

### FOR THE CHICKEN

2 boneless and skinless chicken thighs or I large chicken breast, cut in half and flattened

2 tbsp salt

2 tbsp freshly ground black pepper

2 tsp garlic powder

2 tsp celery salt

Buttermilk

Oil for frying

200g plain flour

100g cornflour

### FOR THE SLAW

2 thin slices of red cabbage

2 thin slices of white cabbage

I carrot

3½ tbsp chilli jam

### FOR THE SAUCE

2-3 tbsp mayo

I-1½ tbsp honey

I-1½ tsp garlic powder

Juice of I lime

### TO BUILD

2 burger buns

2 slices of red Leicester cheese

## HOW YOU DO IT

Get the chicken in a bowl, add half of all the seasonings and mix together so the meat is completely coated. Pour in enough buttermilk to coat the chicken thoroughly and mix it all up again. Cover the bowl and put in the fridge for at least I hour, ideally 24 hours.

While the chicken marinates, make the slaw by shredding the cabbage and carrot into thin strips. Mix the vegetables with the chilli jam to get the sweet flavour coming through evenly. For the sauce, chuck it all in a bowl, mix and leave to one side or in the fridge until everything else is ready.

When the chicken is ready, fill a deep-sided pan with enough oil to pretty much cover the chicken and warm it up. Meanwhile, make the coating by chucking the flour, cornflour and remaining seasoning (salt, pepper, garlic powder, celery salt) into a bowl and mixing well.

When the oil is hot enough, take the chicken one piece at a time out of the buttermilk and place it into the flour coating. Pat down and turn over to make sure it's completely coated, then lower into the hot oil and fry until golden on the outside and cooked through. While the chicken is cooking, toast the buns cut side down in a hot frying pan or under the grill.

When everything's ready, build your burgers up from the bottom like this: bottom bun, chilli jam slaw, fried chicken, slice of cheese (melt this onto the chicken under the grill for a few seconds) and then the top bun, coated on the toasted side with a thick layer of the honey-lime mayo.

# DRUNKEN WALK HOME

Yeah, I know right: them things we like when we're stumbling home from a night out, then you wake up the morning after, see the wrappers on the floor and ask yourself why... Well, here's an awesome burger version using the seasoning they put in kebab shop doner meat.

## YOU NEED

120-220g lamb mince (depending on your preferred patty size, more if you're doubling or tripling up)

2 heaped tbsp doner meat seasoning (I use Tongmaster which you can get online)

2 tbsp kebab shop slaw (see page 141)

I heaped tbsp garlic mayo (see page 139)

I heaped tbsp chilli sauce (Make your own or buy a good bottled one)

I burger bun

2 slices of red Leicester cheese

I pickled jalapeño, sliced

## HOW YOU DO IT

Put the mince in a bowl, add the doner meat seasoning and mix up well, then shape the mix into your burger patty or patties and leave to one side.

Prep the slaw, mayo and chilli sauce if you want to make your own or get the jars/bottles out. Toast the bun, either by grilling it or placing cut side down in a hot frying pan.

If you haven't already, get a frying pan nice and hot (same for the oven if you're using that cooking method) and then cook the patty or patties according to your method of choice (see page 43). Don't forget to cheese them up!

When everything's ready, build your burger from the bottom up in this order: bottom bun, chilli sauce, kebab shop slaw, cheese-topped patty, garlic mayo, pickled chilli (this is optional) and then the top bun.

# EL CHAPO

Mexican grub shoved in a bun that makes you wanna grab your maracas.

## YOU NEED

1 burger bun

1 heaped tbsp guacamole (see page 140)

1 heaped tbsp salsa (Make your own or buy a good jarred one)

1 burger patty (see page 43)

1 slice of Mexican cheese (more if you're doubling or tripling up)

1 jalapeño, sliced (or another large chilli)

4 tortilla chips

## HOW YOU DO IT

Get the bun toasted, either by grilling it or placing cut side down in a hot frying pan. Meanwhile, make the guac and salsa, or use jarred ones, whatever tickles your fancy at the time.

Make up and cook the burger patty according to your method of choice (see page 43) and get the cheese melted on top.

When everything's ready, build your burger from the bottom up in this order: bottom bun, guacamole, sliced chilli, cheese-topped burger patty, tortilla chips, salsa, top bun, and then eat the damn thing.

# FRAZZLE DAZZLE

Pinch your kid's school dinner crisps and use them for something a bit more grown up. Grab a tub of crispy onions from the supermarket if you don't fancy making your own.

## YOU NEED

1 onion, peeled and thinly sliced

1 bottle of Frank's RedHot Buffalo Wings Sauce

100-125g plain flour

1 tbsp salt

1 tbsp ground black pepper

1 tsp garlic granules

250-300ml veg oil

2 beef burger patties (or 1 thick one – see page 43)

2-3 heaped tbsp mayo

12-14 Frazzles

Pinch of Cajun seasoning

Pinch of garlic powder

Pinch of paprika

1 burger bun

2 slices of burger cheese

1 heaped tbsp burger sauce (see page 139)

## HOW YOU DO IT

First, sort the crispy onions. Get the sliced onion in a bowl and pour over the hot sauce, mix well and then slam in the fridge for 20 minutes or so.

Grab another bowl and pour in the flour, salt, pepper and garlic granules, mixing well. Get the oil in a pan and get it hot. Drop the onions into the flour and make sure they're coated before putting them into the oil. Cook until golden and crispy, turning occasionally, then scoop them out, drain and put to one side while you make the burgers.

Whack the oven on to about 220°c if you're making the thicker patty. Get the beef weighed and shaped according to your chosen method, ready for cooking.

Put the mayo in a bowl, crush up about half the Frazzles and then stir them in to make 'frazzinaise'. Add the Cajun seasoning, garlic powder and paprika to taste. Mix it all together and set aside.

Slap a frying pan on a medium-high heat. Grab the bun and toast it cut sides down in the hot pan. Now get your burger patties cooking and when they're nearly ready, melt the cheese on top.

Build your burger from the bottom up in this order: bottom bun, frazzinaise, cheese-topped patties, the rest of the Frazzles and a handful of your crispy onions, then the top bun with burger sauce spread on the inside.

# HONEY CHICK

Sweet and naughty like you always wanted to be.

## YOU NEED

I rasher of smoked bacon

I burger bun

I chicken breast or steak

I heaped tbsp caramelised red onion chutney

I burger patty (see page 43)

2 slices of burger cheese

I heaped tbsp honey mustard sauce

### FOR THE CAJUN HONEY BUTTER

2 heaped tbsp butter

I heaped tbsp honey

I tsp Cajun seasoning

$\frac{1}{8}$ tsp garlic powder

$\frac{1}{4}$ tsp celery salt

## HOW YOU DO IT

Dice the bacon, put into a warm pan and cook until crispy. Remove the bacon from the pan and then add the bun cut side down to toast in the fat. Meanwhile, cut the chicken in half so it can cook more evenly in the pan, butterflying it first if you're using a chicken breast. Chop the crispy bacon and mix it with the caramelised onion chutney.

Mix the butter thoroughly with the honey, Cajun seasoning, garlic powder and celery salt, then rub this all over the chicken to coat it completely. Put the chicken in a medium-hot pan to start cooking.

Meanwhile, sort your burger out and get it cooking according to your chosen method (see page 43). Time it right so that it's ready at the same time as the chicken. Top the patty with the cheese and put under a hot grill to melt.

Now build that mother up: first the bottom bun, then some crispy bacon and caramelised red onion chutney, now your cheese-topped burger patty, then the Cajun honey butter chicken, and finally a nice layer of honey mustard sauce spread on the toasted side of the top bun.

# LAMB ARAYES

This is a Lebanese style burger – basically a grilled, meat-stuffed pitta – for you to get your chops around. Use rectangular pittas if you can so they're easier to cook on all sides.

## YOU NEED

500g lamb mince

1 tbsp tomato purée

1 tbsp salt

1 tbsp black pepper

1 tbsp smoked paprika

1 tbsp onion powder

½ tbsp garlic powder

½ tbsp chilli powder

½ cup very finely chopped fresh parsley or coriander

Grated cheese (optional, just to add a bit more filth)

3 pittas, halved and then quartered if a good size

## HOW YOU DO IT

Combine the mince with the tomato purée, salt, pepper, smoked paprika, onion powder, garlic powder, chilli powder and fresh herbs in a bowl. Mix well to make sure the meat is flavoured evenly. If you want to add cheese, mix some in now.

Get a skillet on a medium heat while you stuff the lamb mixture into each pitta pocket until they're all full. Push the mince down a bit so the pitta isn't flat but not overly chunky either (otherwise they'll take ages to cook). Find the medium you're happy with.

Put the pittas into the skillet meat side down and let them cook for a few minutes. If they're quartered, turn them onto the other meat side and continue cooking until sealed and browned. Now lay them down to toast the pittas on one side, then flip over to do the same again. Repeat this process until the pittas are crispy and the meat inside is cooked, then serve with your choice of dips.

# SIDE CHICK

This chick should always be by your side, spicing up your life and keeping you on your toes.

## YOU NEED

2 pieces of fried chicken (see the Dirty Bird recipe on page 48)

4 rashers of streaky bacon

2 burger buns

2 slices of American burger cheese

2 tbsp cream cheese

1 jalapeño, sliced

Pinch of garlic powder

3-4 tbsp relish

Squirt of hot sauce

## HOW YOU DO IT

Sort the chicken and get it marinating. Meanwhile, get a grill on and line a baking tray with greaseproof paper. Put the bacon on the tray and slam it under the grill, turning when needed, then take out when nice and crispy. Toast the buns under the grill at the same time.

When the chicken is marinated and coated according to the recipe on page 48, get a deep-sided frying pan on the heat and add enough oil to cover nearly all the chicken (or use a deep-fat fryer). Follow the cooking instructions on the recipe and then melt the cheese slices on top of the fried chicken under the grill.

In a small bowl, beat the cream cheese with the jalapeño and garlic powder. Spread this on the toasted side of the top halves of your buns.

Now build this chick from the bottom up like so: bottom bun, relish, cheese-topped fried chicken, crispy bacon, hot sauce and the top bun complete with chilli cheese spread.

# THE GENNARO SAVASTANO

A homage to my favourite character from Gomorrah. If you know, you know.

## YOU NEED

2 tbsp diced pancetta

I heaped tbsp pizza sauce (see page 36)

I heaped tbsp butter

I tsp garlic powder

⅛ tsp dried mixed herbs

I burger bun

I burger patty (see page 43)

I packet of sliced mozzarella

6 slices of good pepperoni (more if you're doubling or tripling up)

Handful of grated mozzarella

Pinch of dried oregano

## HOW YOU DO IT

Fry the pancetta until crispy or pop in a hot oven to cook. Meanwhile, make the pizza sauce and get the garlic butter sorted by mixing the butter, garlic powder and mixed herbs together in a bowl.

In the pan you used to cook the pancetta, toast the bun cut side down in the juices, then spread the garlic butter on both halves and put to one side.

Make up and cook the burger patty according to your method of choice (see page 43) and then melt a slice of the mozzarella on top. Cover that with 3 slices of pepperoni. Repeat if you're having more than one patty.

Put the other 3 slices of pepperoni on the top half of the bun, sprinkle with grated mozzarella and oregano, then stick it under the grill to melt the cheese.

When everything's ready, build your burger from the bottom up in this order: bottom bun, pizza sauce, pancetta, cheese-and-pepperoni-topped patty, more pepperoni, more mozzarella (repeat up to this point if you're making a double or triple burger) and then the top bun, spread with more pizza sauce on the inside. It should look like the picture opposite.

Here I'm just poking you with dirty
sausage goodness. Hot dogs seem to be
breaking out like burgers and fries did
a few years back. I mean, who doesn't
love a good hotdog? It's the smell of
them sizzling on a grill at a fair,
festival or any other event that reels
you in every time, no matter how bad
they are.

Over here we are not blessed with
accessible, quality hotdog sausages
and so the name of the game is to use
whatever sausage you want. It could be a
standard sausage, one from a tin or the
bigger ones in a jar. Some of you might
even manage to blag some proper thick,
long hotdogs from your local butcher.

The same goes for the bun situation.
Generally, we only really find finger
rolls in our shops, but there are hotdog
buns out there. Admittedly, they don't
hold up as well as they should, but they
are there. Go out and find your own buns
that allow your chosen sausage to slide
right in and get covered in filth.

# DIRTY
# DOGS

# BACON WRAPPED CHILLI DOG

**MAKES 4**

A classic dog combo that works every time.

## YOU NEED

280g beef chilli (see page 136)

4 rashers of streaky bacon

4 hotdog sausages

4 buns

Couple handfuls of your favourite grated cheese

1-2 jalapeños, sliced

Ketchup n mustard

## HOW YOU DO IT

First, get your chilli made using the recipe on page 136.

Wrap the bacon around the dogs and get them in a frying pan on a medium heat, with the end of the bacon pan side down to seal the wrap. Turn occasionally until the bacon is cooked how you like it.

## THE BUILD

Get the buns ready and build up your dog like so: dog wrapped in bacon on the bun, spoon in the chilli, sprinkle over the cheese and wedge in the jalapeño slices. Add ketchup n mustard or your choice of sauce on top and serve.

# CHILLI DOG GRILLED CHEESE

Chilli, hotdogs and toasted sarnie? Hell yeah.

## YOU NEED

300g beef chilli (see page 136)
4 rashers of smoked streaky bacon
4 large hotdog sausages, halved
Butter for spreading
4 thick slices of bread
130g Mexicana cheese, grated

## HOW YOU DO IT

Make the chilli according to the recipe on page 136. In the meantime, wrap the streaky bacon around each piece of hotdog. Get a frying pan on a medium-low heat and gently fry the bacon-wrapped dogs, with the end of the bacon pan side down to seal the wrap. Turn occasionally until cooked to your liking.

Spread the butter on one side of the sliced bread. When everything is ready, build it up like this: put the first slice of bread butter side down, sprinkle on some the cheese and spoon on some beef chilli. Then, lay the dogs lengthways on the bread so they're arranged vertically from the top to the bottom of the slice. Add more chilli over the top and then the rest of the cheese. Place another slice of bread on top with the butter side facing up. Repeat to make the second sandwich.

Place your sandwiches into the frying pan on a medium-low heat and cook until the buttered side of the bread is golden and the cheese starts to melt. Flip and do the same on the other side, pushing down a bit. When the outer bits look golden and crispy and the cheese has melted, remove from the heat, cut in half and serve.

# DOG BITES

These only bark and don't bite, but they're fun to make and munch on.

## YOU NEED

6 slices of white bread

Ketchup n mustard

6-8 slices of burger cheese, or your choice of grated cheese

6 hotdog sausages

Oil or cooking spray

Shallow bowl of milk

Crispy onions

## HOW YOU DO IT

Slap the oven on to around 200°c. Cut all the crusts off each slice of bread. One at a time, put the bread on a flat surface and use a rolling pin to flatten and stretch it out a bit. Now for the messy part... Gently rub one side of each slice just to make the bread coarse instead of smooth again. Squirt some ketchup and mustard on this side and add the cheese. Put a hotdog on one end of the slice and then roll up the bread until it looks like a sausage roll.

Coat a baking tray with some oil or cooking spray and warm it up in the oven. Dunk the dog bites into the bowl of milk to briefly soak the bread and then put them onto the tray with the join underneath to seal the rolls. Cook until golden, then transfer to a plate and cut them in half if you like, or leave them whole. Sprinkle over the crispy onions, squirt on more sauce and enjoy.

# FAT DOG

Fully loaded and should be overflowing for full effect.

## YOU NEED

6 slices of streaky bacon, smoked or unsmoked

2 boneless skinless chicken thighs

2 tbsp salt

2 tbsp pepper

2 tsp garlic powder

300ml buttermilk

75g plain flour

30g cornflour

Oil for frying

250g beef mince

3 slices of burger cheese

8 tbsp mac n cheese (see page 134)

4 hotdogs of your choice

4 buns

Couple handfuls of crispy onions

Burger sauce (see page 139)

## HOW YOU DO IT

Fry, grill or oven bake the bacon until crispy then chop it up into bits. Meanwhile, put the chicken, salt, pepper and garlic powder in a bowl, coating the chicken well. Pour enough buttermilk over the chicken to coat thoroughly, mix it all together and put in the fridge to marinate for at least an hour.

When the chicken is ready, mix the flour and cornflour together in a bowl with a bit of salt, pepper and garlic powder, mixing well. Take the chicken out of the marinade and coat the pieces in a nice even layer of the seasoned flour.

Get a pan on a high heat with enough oil to shallow or deep fry the chicken. Add the chicken to the hot pan and cook until golden and crispy.

Heat up another frying pan and get the mince cooked until brown. Add a pinch of salt n pepper to season the beef and stir in. Lay the burger cheese on top of the meat and when the cheese has melted, stir it all in. Meanwhile, heat up the mac n cheese and cook your hotdogs in the usual way.

## THE BUILD

Now you're ready to make a Fat Dog. Build it up like this: bun, hotdog, cheesy beef, fried chicken, mac n cheese, bacon bits, crispy onions, burger sauce.

# MAC DOG

Hotdogs with mac n cheese are a great combo for your filthy lips.

## YOU NEED

4 tbsp mac n cheese (see page 134)

4 rashers of streaky bacon

2 rashers of smoked streaky bacon

2 hotdog sausages

2 buns

Crispy onions

BBQ sauce

## HOW YOU DO IT

Fry off the streaky bacon and when it's nice and crispy, chop it up and put it to one side. Wrap a rasher of the smoked streaky bacon around each of the hotdogs. Put these in a frying pan on a medium-high heat, with the overlapping bit of bacon underneath so the direct heat can seal it. Keep turning until the bacon is cooked how you like it. Meanwhile, heat up the mac n cheese.

When everything is done, build the dog like so: bun, bacon-wrapped dog, mac n cheese (don't be shy with spooning this in) and then a sprinkle of bacon bits and crispy onions. Squirt over some barbecue sauce for that extra filth.

Loaded fries are all the rage right now. Not only do they taste good, but they're also photogenic, plus the beauty of fries is that you can do pretty much anything with them and they still do the job. You could probably chuck soup over them and get away with it. Thankfully, we're not doing that here.

There's a whole range of different chips n fries, as you'll see on the following pages. It's entirely up to you what you want to use for each dish. I'll be using a variety here just to show you it really doesn't matter what you use.

Again, what's coming up are just some ideas for you to build on to your own liking. You can use a deep fryer, air fryer or an oven for any of these. It's down to your preference at the time of making them. At the end of the day, a chip is a chip. It's all made of the same stuff, and it all goes down the same hatch. Ideally, you'll want your fries to be crispy on the outside but soft and fluffy in the middle. As we're loading them up with all manner of things, having them crispy to start with definitely helps.

# LOADED FRIES

# CARNE ASADA FRIES

These are just awesome. Nuff said.

## YOU NEED

2 portions of fries

Oil or cooking spray

250g beef or lamb mince (or both)

Pinch of salt n pepper

1-2 tbsp fajita seasoning

3-4 tbsp salsa (Make your own or buy a good jarred one)

Chimichurri mayo (see page 141)

Garlic mayo (see page 139 or use a bottled one)

2 piquanté peppers, thinly sliced widthways

## HOW YOU DO IT

Slap your fries on and get them cooked. Meanwhile, squirt a bit of oil or cooking spray into a frying pan on a high heat. Grab the mince and add it to the hot frying pan. Cook until brown, then add the salt, pepper and fajita seasoning, stirring well and tasting as you go. Add extra seasoning if you like.

Grab a big mixing bowl, chuck in the hot fries and the salsa, then mix together well.

## THE BUILD

Divide the salsa coated fries between your bowls or plates. Spoon the mince on top, then add a good layer of the chimichurri mayo and a drizzle of garlic mayo. Scatter the peppers on top and serve.

# CHEESE SAUCE FRIES

A staple combination.

## YOU NEED

2 portions of fries

300ml double cream

Good handful of grated red Leicester

4 slices of burger cheese, ripped into pieces

## HOW YOU DO IT

Slap your fries into a pan and get them cooking. For the cheese sauce, put a saucepan on a medium heat. Pour in the double cream and get it hot, but not boiling or simmering. Chuck in all the cheeses and stir until melted and the sauce has a nice, thickish consistency.

Divide your fries between plates or bowls and pour the cheese sauce over the top. Serve up and sprinkle over any toppings you want (or none, if you prefer). These can be crispy onion bits, crispy chopped bacon, diced steak, chicken... basically anything. Use your imagination and get dirty with it.

# CHICK N STEAK FRIES

Basically, a cowboy's surf n turf. Let's face it, cowboys eat meat not stuff from the sea.

## YOU NEED

2 portions of fries

1-2 marbled steaks (approx. 200g each)

Hot sauce (like Reds Wing Sauce)

## FOR THE CHICKEN

400g chicken (boneless & skinless thighs, or breast cut into strips)

2 tsp salt

2 tsp ground black pepper

2 tsp garlic powder

150ml buttermilk

200g plain flour

100g cornflour

## FOR THE HONEY N GARLIC SAUCE

2 tbsp olive oil

3 cloves of garlic, minced

60ml soy sauce

250ml honey

## HOW YOU DO IT

First off, sort the chicken out by seasoning it with half of the salt, pepper and garlic powder in a large bowl. Add the buttermilk and mix everything up, ensuring the chicken is fully coated. Leave it overnight, or for at least an hour, in the fridge.

When you're ready to get cooking, heat a small saucepan and add the olive oil for the honey n garlic sauce. Add the minced garlic and cook for a couple of minutes, making sure you don't burn it. Stir in the soy sauce and honey, then let the sauce simmer for 5 minutes. Transfer the sauce into a bowl and leave it to cool.

Now get the fries going and pour enough oil into a pan over a medium heat to shallow fry the chicken. Meanwhile, put the flour, cornflour and remaining seasoning (salt, pepper and garlic powder) in another bowl and give it a good mix.

Drop each piece of the marinated chicken into the flour and pat it down, making sure it's fully coated. Then lower the chicken into the hot oil to fry, turning as you go until it's all cooked and has a nice golden crust on the outside. When ready, take it out and drain off the excess oil.

While you're frying the chicken, you can cook the steak to your liking, then let it rest before slicing however you prefer.

Now to build these bad boys. Pile your fries onto a plate or bowl, then add the fried chicken on one side and the steak on the other. Drizzle over the honey n garlic sauce you made and some hot sauce.

Eat it. Eat it now, damn it!

# FONDUE FRIES

Because you're posh and want to be different...

## YOU NEED

2 portions of fries

5 slices of smoked streaky bacon

170-200g Gruyère

160-180g Brie

4 slices of American burger cheese

Pinch of smoked paprika

Pinch of oregano

## HOW YOU DO IT

Get the fries cooking and once they're not far off, get the grill on. Line a pan with greaseproof paper, lay the bacon onto it and put under the hot grill to cook. When done, chop it up and set to one side.

Meanwhile, get a saucepan on a medium-low heat. Add all the cheeses, stirring occasionally until they've melted.

## THE BUILD

Empty the fries into your eating vessels. Pour over the cheese fondue and then scatter the bacon pieces on top. Sprinkle over the smoked paprika and oregano, then serve.

# GAMBINO FRIES

If they ain't running New York, they're running the fry business. So, here's an offer you can't refuse.

## YOU NEED

2 large slices of pancetta

½ onion, finely chopped

250g beef mince

2 cloves of garlic, minced

½ tbsp tomato purée

1 x 400g tin of chopped tomatoes

1 tbsp Italian mixed herbs

Salt n pepper

3-4 tbsp grated parmesan

2 portions of curly fries

Couple handfuls of grated mozzarella

Dried oregano, to taste

## HOW YOU DO IT

Cook the pancetta under a grill or in a frying pan until crispy. Chop into bits and put to one side.

Make the Bolognese by lobbing the onion into a pan on a medium heat and cooking until soft. Next, add the mince and cook until brown. Add the garlic and tom purée, give it a mix while it cooks down a bit, then pour in the tinned tomatoes and mixed herbs. Stir to combine and then let the sauce simmer until it reduces by two thirds.

Once the sauce has reduced, add salt n pepper and anything else you like for extra flavour. Chuck in some parmesan and mix it up. Meanwhile, get the fries cooking in whatever way you want to.

## THE BUILD

When the fries are ready, you can build the Gambino Fries and it goes like this: fries, Bolognese sauce, sprinkle of parmesan, handful of grated mozza, sprinkle of oregano, crispy pancetta bits. Let the mozza melt into the Bolognese and you have a winner.

# MEXICALI FRIES

Kinda like a Mexican stir-fry type thing on fries.

## YOU NEED

2 portions of fries

2 chicken breasts or 2 nice steaks, cut into strips

1 tbsp Cajun seasoning, plus extra to finish

¼ tbsp garlic powder

⅛ tbsp salt n pepper

⅛ onion, finely sliced

¼ red pepper, cut into thin strips

¼ green pepper, cut into thin strips

¼ yellow or orange pepper, cut into thin strips

Jalapeños or roquito peppers, thinly sliced into rings

American mustard (like French's)

Garlic mayo (see page 139)

## HOW YOU DO IT

Get your choice of fries cooking. Cut the chicken or steak (or both) into strips and then coat the meat with the Cajun seasoning, garlic powder and salt n pepper. Get a frying pan hot and add the meat. Once it's cooked, add the onion, pepper and chilli. Keep cooking until the vegetables are done. If the mix dries out, add a bit of water where needed.

Meanwhile, mix some Cajun seasoning and salt together. When they're ready, put the fries in a big bowl and sprinkle the Cajun salt over them. Mix up to taste, then portion the fries out into serving bowls, or one big dish if you're sharing. Add the meat mixture, drizzle your sauces on top and dig in.

# MOU LING (DRUNKEN MONKEY) FRIES

A popular Thai dish, pad krapow, on fries. I guess that makes this some kind of fusion food.

## YOU NEED

2 portions of fries

⅛ onion, finely chopped

4 cloves of garlic, finely chopped

8 bird's eye chillies, finely chopped

220g chicken, cut into thin strips

Soy sauce to taste

Good splash of oyster sauce

Good splash of fish sauce

Good bunch of fresh basil

2 eggs

Pinch of finely chopped coriander

Squirt of chilli mayo

Squirt of garlic mayo (see page 139)

## HOW YOU DO IT

Get the chips cooking. Have a frying pan or wok at the ready and get it hot. Chuck in a splash of oil, then add the onion, garlic and chilli and prepare to sneeze.

Add the chicken strips and mix it all together. Stir in the soy, oyster and fish sauces. Keep cooking and mixing it up. If it's going dry, add a bit of water.

At the last minute, add the basil to your wok and mix it all up until the basil has wilted. While you do that, fry the eggs in a separate pan until cooked to your liking.

Get the fries into a bowl or plate and then spoon the chicken mixture over the top. Add your fried eggs and sprinkle over the chopped coriander, then finish with the sauces.

# NORMAL FRIES

When I had my burger place, people would always ask for "normal fries." We would always say that we'd love to do some really expensive loaded fries called normal fries and it'd stop people asking for them. Never got round to it, but here's some un-expensive normal fries.

## YOU NEED

2 pieces of buttermilk fried chicken (see page 82)

6 slices of smoked streaky bacon

2 portions of fries

2 tbsp salt

2 tbsp ground black pepper

Garlic mayo (see page 139)

Good squirt of hot sauce

Good squirt of BBQ sauce

Grated hard cheese (like parmesan)

## HOW YOU DO IT

To get the chicken prepped, follow the Chick n Steak Fries recipe on page 82. You might want to do this the night before. When it's marinated, get the oven or grill on and line a tray with greaseproof paper. Lay the bacon out and get it cooking, turning when needed. Get your choice of fries ready in your usual way.

Go back to the chicken and follow the recipe to get it coated and cooked. When the fries are ready, chuck them into a big bowl, add the salt n pepper and toss until the fries are coated. Pour them onto your serving plates or bowls.

## THE BUILD

Chop up the crispy bacon and scatter it over the fries. Slice the fried chicken widthways and lay it out on top. Drizzle over the garlic mayo, hot sauce and the BBQ sauce. Finish by sprinkling over the grated cheese.

# PIZZA FRIES

You normally have fries as a side with pizza, right? Well now you can have the pizza on the fries.

## YOU NEED

2 portions of fries

Salt n pepper to taste

Pizza sauce (optional, see page 36)

2 good handfuls of grated mozzarella

12 pepperoni slices

3 tbsp grated hard cheese (like parmesan)

Pinch of dried oregano

## HOW YOU DO IT

Get the oven or grill warming up and when it's hot, start cooking the fries. When the fries are ready, toss with salt n pepper in a bowl to make sure they're fully seasoned. If you're sharing, you can put the fries into one big serving dish or divide them between bowls if not (use something ovenproof).

## THE BUILD

If using, reheat your pizza sauce and then spoon it over the fries, followed by the mozzarella, pepperoni, hard cheese and oregano. Put them in the oven or under a grill to let the cheese melt. Take out and get scoffing.

I know what you're thinking... it's not
that kind: it's about stuff slapped in
bread and on it but still being just as
naughty as what you were originally
thinking.

Who discovered bread? I mean, it's like
the person who discovered honey by
sitting staring at a bee's nest and
had that lightbulb moment of "there's
something bloody nice in there, I know
it." Someone must have been staring at
grains and thought "if I grind this up,
it's gonna turn into something I can
use to make an endless possibility of
food with..." Well, whoever it was gave us
a never-ending treat that we can use to
make all manner of filthy grub.

It's unreal how many different types of
bread are out there now but fear not:
we're not going to get fancy with far-
out breads that we don't understand.
We're using normal bread, but if you
wanna change it up, feel free to crack
on, no one's stopping you.

The beauty of bread is that you can
cook it in a lot of different ways and it
still pretty much comes out the same.
Plus, it's awesome with messy treats
stuffed inside for you to munch down
on.

Let's take a look at what we can knock
up, shall we?

# BEEFY MAC WRAP

Beef, mac n cheese and other stuff always go together like carrots and peas.

## YOU NEED

1 tbsp salt

1 tbsp ground black pepper

4 beef steak medallions

3-4 rashers of streaky bacon

Mac n cheese (see page 134 but double the recipe)

Knob of butter

Sprinkle of garlic powder

Sprinkle of dried thyme or rosemary

Squirt of hot mayo

2 large tortilla wraps

2-3 tbsp crispy onions (homemade or from a tub)

## HOW YOU DO IT

Mix the salt and pepper together in a bowl, then coat the beef medallions all over with the seasoning. Cook the streaky bacon until nice and crispy, then dice it up. Make the mac n cheese.

Cook the medallions in a hot pan with the butter, garlic and herbs until done to your crookedness, then take out and leave to rest while you squirt the hot mayo over the tortillas.

Slice the rested beef into thin strips, place some in the middle of each tortilla, spoon on your mac n cheese to one side of the beef, sprinkle on the crispy onions and wrap.

Put the filled wraps in a medium-hot frying pan with the fold underneath to seal it. Cut the wraps in half and serve with hot sauce and chimichurri, or any sauces you like.

# CHICKEN HERO GRILLED CHEESE

A dirty chicken sandwich that your local lunchtime grub wagon doesn't do.

## YOU NEED

100g breadcrumbs

1 tbsp salt

1 tbsp ground black pepper

1 egg

50g plain flour

2 chicken steaks

Oil for shallow frying the chicken

Butter for spreading

4 thickish slices of bread

4 slices of burger cheese

4 slices of streaky bacon, cooked and chopped up

Couple handfuls of grated mozzarella

Parmesan or other hard cheese, grated

4 slices of smoked cheese

## HOW YOU DO IT

Mix the breadcrumbs with the salt n pepper in one bowl. Crack the egg into a second bowl and beat, then put the flour in a third bowl. Dunk the chicken in this order: flour, egg, flour again, egg again, and then the seasoned breadcrumbs. Ensure the chicken is completely coated.

Heat the oil in a pan on a medium-high heat and fry the coated chicken steaks until golden, crispy and cooked though.

While the chicken is cooking, spread one side of each slice of bread with butter. Once the chicken is ready, you can build the sandwich like so: first slice of bread (with the buttered side facing outwards), 2 slices of burger cheese, bacon, chicken, mozzarella, hard cheese, 2 slices of smoked cheese, and then another slice of bread (again with the buttered side out). Repeat to make the second sandwich.

Now get a pan on a medium heat and place the sandwich in butter side down. When golden, flip over and cook on the other side. Watch for the cheese to melt inside and the outsides to turn golden. Once done, cut the grilled cheese in half and serve with any sauce of your choice, or no sauce... however you like it, just sink your face into it.

# CHICKEN PARM SCHNITZEL SLIDERS

SERVES 6-8

These are just awesome. Nuff said.

## YOU NEED

1 French stick

Knob of butter

1⅛ tsp garlic powder

1 tsp mixed herbs

2 eggs, beaten

150g plain flour

150g breadcrumbs

1 tsp celery salt

1 tsp salt

1 tsp pepper

2 tbsp grated parmesan

Oil for shallow frying

3-4 chicken steaks

Pizza sauce (see page 36 but double or triple the recipe)

2 good handfuls of grated red cheese

2 good handfuls of grated mozzarella cheese

1-2 tbsp dried oregano

### FOR THE WHITE SAUCE

(or use one from a jar)

2 heaped tbsp butter

3 tbsp plain flour

350ml milk

Big handful of grated cheddar

2 tbsp grated parmesan

## HOW YOU DO IT

First, make the white sauce. Melt the butter in a saucepan over a medium heat, then add the flour and stir to form a smooth paste. Add the milk and whisk constantly until there are no lumps, then throw in the cheeses and stir until melted. Let the sauce cook until it thickens (not overly thick but nowhere near runny) and then put to one side until needed.

Preheat the oven to 220°c. Cut the French stick into approximately 8cm pieces that will fit closely together on a baking tray. Slice each piece in half horizontally and put the bottom halves on the tray, keeping them close together, then set the top halves to one side.

Beat the butter with the garlic powder and mixed herbs in a small bowl. Now grab three more bowls and put the eggs in the first, the flour in the second, and the breadcrumbs in the third. Mix the celery salt, salt n pepper, a pinch of garlic powder and 1 tablespoon of the grated parmesan into the breadcrumbs.

Get a pan on a medium-high heat and fill it with enough oil to cover the chicken. Dip the steaks into the bowls in this order: flour, egg, flour again, egg again, and then the seasoned breadcrumbs. Make sure each piece is completely coated before putting it into the oil. Turn the sizzling chicken over occasionally until it's cooked through and the coating is golden and crispy. Drain the schnitzel on kitchen roll to soak up the excess oil.

Grab the bread tray and spread the garlic butter over the bottom halves. Pour over the pizza sauce so it covers the bread. Cut the chicken schnitzel into pieces to fit the bread and lay them on top of the sauce. Spoon over the white sauce, sprinkle with the cheeses and oregano, then put the top halves on each slider and stick the tray in the hot oven. Cook until all the cheese melts (about 15-20 minutes) before eating.

# COLD CUT GRILLED CHEESE

A selection of meats, cheese and pesto. Mix it up using different meats and keep enjoying it.

## YOU NEED

2 thick self-cut slices of crusty bread

Butter for spreading

$1\frac{1}{2}$ - 2 tbsp green pesto

$1\frac{1}{2}$ - 2 tbsp red pesto

I large ball of good quality mozzarella

Handful of grated red cheese

Handful of pulled ham hock

4-5 slices of pastrami

2 slices of smoked ham

## HOW YOU DO IT

Heat up the oven to about 220°c. Spread the slices of bread with butter on one side and pesto on the other. Place both slices butter side down so the pesto is facing up.

For the filling, slice the mozzarella and layer it on what will be the top slice of bread. Sprinkle some of the grated red cheese on top, then slap all the meat on the other slice. Sandwich the two slices together so the buttered sides are facing outwards.

Warm up a frying pan on a medium heat, then put the sandwich in to cook. Flip over and cook on the other side when golden, pushing down a bit to stick everything together. When the bread is nice and golden on the outside and the cheese melts and oozes on the inside, the toastie is ready. Cut into quarters or halves and serve.

# DIRTY STEAK BAGUETTE

Because every cookbook needs its own version, right?

## YOU NEED

1 medium onion

1 bottle of Birra Moretti

Knob of butter

1 tsp sugar

1 stone-baked baguette (or a French stick)

1 nicely marbled ribeye or sirloin steak

Salt n pepper to taste

1½ tbsp butter

1 sprig of fresh thyme or 1 tsp dried thyme

2-3 cloves of garlic, peeled and lightly crushed

Handful of mixed salad leaves

Chimichurri mayo (see page 141)

## HOW YOU DO IT

Thinly slice the onion, pop into a bowl and cover with the beer. Leave this to marinate for an hour. Get a pan on a medium heat, drain the beery onions and then cook for a few minutes until soft. Add the butter and sugar, then continue frying until the onions have started to caramelise. Tip them into a bowl and put to one side.

Toast the baguette – I slap it in the oven at 220°c for a bit, turning when needed – and get the frying pan piping hot. Put the steak into the pan and season the top side with salt n pepper. When the steak has a good crust, flip it over and season again. Add the butter, thyme and garlic to the pan, then start spooning the flavoured butter over the steak (basting) and rubbing the garlic cloves into it.

When the steak is cooked to just under how you normally like it, take it out of the pan and let it rest on a chopping board for 5 minutes. The steak will keep cooking while it rests. Meanwhile, spread a bit of butter inside the baguette, cover the bottom half with salad leaves and your caramelised onions, then slice up and layer on the steak. Add a good layer of chimichurri mayo, then cut in half or into three and get munching on that goodness.

# FISHY FINGER IN A JOE EXOTIC BUN

Something fishy from the Tiger King...

## YOU NEED

2 crusty tiger rolls

2 boneless and skinless white fish fillets (like cod)

Frozen, tinned or fresh garden peas

Knob of butter

Fresh mint (optional)

### FOR THE BATTER

200g plain flour

150ml good ale

50ml sparkling water

½ tsp bicarbonate of soda

Good pinch of salt n pepper

Pinch of ground turmeric

### FOR THE TARTARE SAUCE

½ cup (approx. 100g) mayo

1 dill pickle, finely chopped

1 tbsp finely chopped fresh parsley

Squeeze of lemon juice

Pinch of salt n pepper

## HOW YOU DO IT

First off, get a deep-sided frying pan or saucepan and put enough oil in to cover the fish once it's prepped. Use a deep-fat fryer if you have one. Either way, get the oil hot enough to cook battered fish.

Cut the fish into pieces just a bit bigger than the buns (you can have them fitting neatly inside or hanging out at either end, the choice is yours). Grab a bowl, put all the ingredients for the batter in and give them a good whisk. The mix should be smooth and pretty thick, not watery or overly runny.

Make the tartare sauce by mixing all the ingredients together in a bowl. Add more seasoning if needed and then leave to one side while you do the cooking.

Get the peas warmed up in a saucepan and then drain off any liquid. Add the butter and mash them up, seasoning with salt and pepper, finely chopped fresh mint or whatever you like.

Dunk the fish in the batter, making sure it's completely coated, and then transfer straight into the hot oil. Turn the pieces occasionally and cook until they are floating and the batter is nice and golden.

Now everything's ready, build your burger from the bottom up in this order in the crusty rolls: mushy peas, battered fish and then a heaped tablespoon of tartare sauce.

# GOOEY BREAD BOWLS WITH TWISTED BACON DIPPERS

Sack off the spoons and use bacon instead because you're a rebel.

## YOU NEED

10-12 thick rashers of bacon (smoked or unsmoked)

2 medium-large crusty rolls

250g cream cheese

1 tsp Cajun seasoning

¼ tsp garlic powder

¼ tsp paprika

Squeeze of lemon juice

Couple handfuls of spinach, wilted and chopped

⅛ small onion, finely chopped

175g mozzarella, grated

50g cheddar, grated

3 slices of Mexicana cheese, finely chopped (or 50g grated)

## HOW YOU DO IT

First off, get the oven on at about 200°c. Prep the bacon by twisting it lengthways, holding one side down and using the other hand to twist it up. Lay the bacon on a baking tray lined with greaseproof paper and whack it in the hot oven, turning occasionally until it's all crisp on the outside.

In the meantime, grab the rolls and cut the tops off so you can hollow the rolls out. Put all the other ingredients into a bowl and mix well, adding extra seasoning to taste.

Spoon the cheesy mixture into the rolls, filling them right to the top so they're stuffed and then slap them in the oven for about 45-60 minutes, or until the cheese has melted and gone gooey in the middle. Take out of the oven and serve hot with the bacon dippers.

# GORDITA

A dirty take on a Mexican street food. Pure filth these are.

## YOU NEED

400g beef mince

⅛ onion, finely chopped

2 cloves of garlic, finely chopped

1⅛ tsp ground cumin

1⅛ tsp ground coriander

1⅛ tsp ground cinnamon

2 tsp chilli powder

2 tsp tomato purée

Glug of red wine

1 x 400g tin of chopped tomatoes

2 large tortilla wraps

Couple handfuls of grated mozzarella

Couple handfuls of grated Mexicana cheese

4 hard taco shells

6-8 tbsp guacamole (see page 140)

6-8 tbsp sour cream

## HOW YOU DO IT

First off, you want to make the chilli. Get a pan on a medium heat, then add the mince and cook until brown. Add the onion and garlic and cook for a further 5 minutes. Next, add the cumin, coriander, cinnamon and chilli powder and stir it all together. Add the tomato purée and red wine, mixing it in and leaving to simmer until the wine reduces. Chuck in the tinned tomatoes, stirring them in and leaving to simmer for 15-20 minutes on a medium heat. Give it a taste and add more seasoning if you feel like it's needed.

When the chilli is nearly ready, whack a frying pan on a medium heat. Grab a tortilla and put it in the pan. As soon as it touches the pan, get a good handful of each cheese and spread them out over the tortilla. Cook the cheesy tortilla until it has started to melt properly.

Break the crispy taco shells in half, scattering them over the melted cheese. Spoon on the chilli, then add dollops of the guac, sour cream, and more cheese. Fold the tortilla in half, then leave it to cook on one side for a minute or so before flipping it over to cook for a final minute. Repeat the process to make a second gordita with the remaining ingredients. Take out of the pan and cut into three or four sections to serve.

# ULTIMATE TOASTIE

Who doesn't love a good toasted sarnie? They're even better when fully loaded with messy treats.

## YOU NEED

7-8 potato puffs

4 rashers of crispy streaky bacon, diced up

1 bloomer loaf (uncut)

Butter for spreading

Good sprinkle of grated cheese (here I'm using a bit of red cheese, mozzarella and smoked applewood)

1 egg

Burger sauce (see page 139)

## HOW YOU DO IT

Get the oven warmed up to 200°c and put the potato puffs in to cook, turning halfway through. If you've not already done the streaky bacon, get that cooked in a pan and diced.

Cut 2 nice slices of the bread. On one slice, cut a hole in the middle. The hole doesn't need to be massive, but big enough to hold a fried egg (about 5cm). Butter one side of each slice.

Warm up a frying pan on a medium heat and when hot, put both pieces of bread in the pan butter side down. Sprinkle a bit of grated cheese into the hole and crack in the egg on top. Sprinkle the cheeses and crispy bacon over the rest of the bread while it cooks for a few minutes until golden underneath and the egg is sealed on the bottom.

Very carefully move the cheesy slice to a baking tray or put your pan into the oven if it's ovenproof. Be careful not to ruin the egg. Sprinkle on a bit more cheese and leave in the hot oven for about 5 minutes while the egg finishes cooking.

Bring it out the oven, squirt burger sauce over the bread, then layer the potato puffs on the non-egg slice of bread. Get the slice with the egg in and put it on top to make the sandwich, then cut through the middle (you'll see where the egg is as it'll have a sealed part on the bread) and the yolk should flow out and you can dig in.

Who doesn't love a good pie? Thing is, I find the usual choice a bit boring; they're all the same flavour fillings and there's never really anything out there that's... well, out there. So, here are some pies that are pure filth. You may want one with mash, you may want one with chips, or you can have any of them with whatever you want: that's the point in these pies. They're different but dead easy to make.

Ideally, for this section you'll want a pie maker. It's honestly one of the best pieces of cooking equipment I've ever had, only costs about £25-35 and you get awesome results. They usually make 2 individual pies so if you're using moulds instead, just pick your preferred size and cut the pastry accordingly.

Now, I've never been great at pastry – it's never been my strong point – so I'm not going to put a recipe in here for pastry, as it'll probably be crap. What I am giving you are recipes for bloody tasty and unique pie fillings, using shop-bought ready-rolled shortcrust pastry, just because it's easier and that's what this book is about: using what you can buy in a supermarket, and working for all skill levels. You can make your own pastry if you want though; as with everything in this book, it's entirely your choice.

You'll want to eat these pies right away while they're hot... just saying.

# PHAAT PIES

# BANGERS N MASH PIE

Two classic English dishes coming together like a boss.

## YOU NEED

2 medium potatoes

Knob of butter

Salt n pepper

Handful of grated cheddar cheese

3-4 good sausages (ideally at least 95% meat)

½ onion, diced

2 tbsp beef gravy granules (I use Bisto)

250ml boiling water

½ a beef stock cube or stock pot

1 sheet of ready-rolled shortcrust pastry

Pie maker or moulds

## HOW YOU DO IT

Peel the spuds, cut them into small cubes and get them boiling in a pan of water until nice and soft. Drain and mash with the knob of butter and some pepper, then add the grated cheddar and make sure everything is mixed well.

While the potatoes are boiling, get the sausages cooked and soften the diced onion in a frying pan with a little oil or butter. When the sausages are cooked, chop them into chunks and mix them with the onion. Dissolve the gravy granules in the boiling water, then add the stock (crumbling it first if using a cube) and pour the mixture into the pan of onion and sausage. Add salt and pepper to taste.

Get the pastry out the fridge and cut to size for the pie maker or your pie moulds. Create the pastry cases and then spoon in the sausage and gravy filling. Put as much mash on top as you can and spread it out before putting the rest of the pastry on top to form the lids. Trim and press the edges together if needed to seal the filling in.

If using a pie maker, close the lid tight, turn it on and wait for it to cook. If using a pie dish or mould, cook the pies in the oven as you would normally.

# CMC PIE BITES

AKA cheeseburger mac n cheese bites. Little pies for big mouths to chomp on time and time again.

## YOU NEED

Deep muffin tray

Soft butter, for greasing

2 sheets of ready-rolled shortcrust pastry

3 rashers of streaky bacon

450g beef mince

2 tbsp tomato purée

Good squirt of hot sauce

Good squirt of American mustard

4 slices of pickle, finely chopped

Pinch of salt n pepper

Handful of grated red Leicester

Handful of grated mozzarella

### FOR THE TOPPING

Few cupfuls of macaroni (you want enough to fill the sauce)

300ml double cream

2 slices of burger cheese

Handful of grated red Leicester

½ handful of grated mozzarella

1-2 tbsp grated parmesan

### TO FINISH

Grated parmesan

Breadcrumbs

Paprika

## HOW YOU DO IT

Whack the oven on to about 200°c. Get a deep muffin tray that has at least 6 sections and wipe them with butter. Cut the pastry to size (I used a normal cereal bowl to cut round) and line the buttered sections so it covers the base and sides. Blind bake for 10-12 minutes using greaseproof paper and baking balls to stop the pastry on the bottom puffing up.

Meanwhile, get the bacon cooked until crispy and then chopped up fairly fine. Put the same pan on a medium-high heat and throw in the mince so it starts to brown. Chuck in the purée, hot sauce, mustard, pickles, salt n pepper and mix everything up. Add more of whatever you want to get the flavour you like. Stir in the grated cheeses and when melted, take the pan off the heat.

## FOR THE TOPPING

Make the mac n cheese by getting a saucepan of boiling water going to cook the macaroni and simmer until just done. At the same time, get the cheese sauce going by putting the cream into a saucepan and when it's warm enough (not boiling or simmering) chuck all the cheeses in and stir until melted. The sauce should be a good thick consistency so if it's not thick enough, lob more cheese in. Drain the cooked pasta and stir into the sauce.

## TO FINISH

Line a baking tray with greaseproof paper and put the baked pastry cases onto it. Spoon the burger mix in, then cover with the mac n cheese. Sprinkle parmesan, breadcrumbs and a bit of paprika over the top of each one. Pop the pie bites back in the oven for another 10-12 minutes or so before serving.

# GREASY SPOON PIE

Breakfast + pie... what can go wrong? Nothing, absolutely nothing.

## YOU NEED

3 large good quality sausages

3 good slices of black pudding

2 full strips of streaky bacon

2 button mushrooms, thinly sliced

1 sheet of ready-rolled shortcrust pasty

$\frac{1}{8}$ tin of baked beans

2 eggs

Pie maker or moulds

## HOW YOU DO IT

Get a frying pan on a medium heat, slice the sausages into chunks and chuck them in the frying pan to cook. Add the black pudding and bacon to cook until crispy, then sauté the mushrooms until soft.

When everything is done to your liking, chop the black pudding and bacon up. Cut the pastry to size and line the pie maker or your pie moulds with it, then layer up the filling. Start with a few chunks of sausage along with some mushrooms, then spoon in some beans. Add more sausage, mushrooms and the bacon, then add the rest of the beans. Make sure you have enough sauce going in with the beans.

Crack the eggs onto the filling with the yolks sitting nicely on top. Put the rest of the pastry on top to make the lids, being careful not to break the yolk. Close the lid and turn on the pie maker or stick the moulds in a hot oven and cook for about 17-18 minutes.

When the pies are ready, take out and cut through the middle so the egg yolk runs down over the messy deliciousness inside. Enjoy.

# LASAGNE PIE

## Because why the hell not?

## YOU NEED

### FOR THE WHITE SAUCE

1½ heaped tbsp butter

I tbsp plain flour

175ml milk

I tbsp grated parmesan

### FOR THE BOLOGNESE

100g beef mince

100g pork mince

I tbsp tomato purée

Splash of red wine

I tin of chopped tomatoes

2 cloves of garlic, minced

⅛ tbsp dried mixed Italian herbs

Salt n pepper to taste

### TO BUILD THE PIE

I sheet of ready-rolled shortcrust pastry

I fresh lasagne sheet

Grated parmesan

Grated mozzarella

Pie maker or moulds

## HOW YOU DO IT

### FOR THE WHITE SAUCE

Get a saucepan on a medium heat, add the butter, let it melt and then add the flour. Mix it up into a soft paste and then gradually stir in the milk. Keep stirring until the roux has liquified, then add the cheese and keep stirring until it thickens slightly. Set aside while you make the bolognese.

### FOR THE BOLOGNESE

Grab a pan and fry the mince on a medium-high heat. Stir until browned, then add the tomato purée and wine. Let it simmer for a couple minutes, then throw in the tinned tomatoes, garlic and mixed herbs. Simmer for 10-15 minutes until the sauce has reduced a good amount. Add salt and pepper to taste, then take off the heat.

If using your oven and moulds to cook the pie, preheat your oven to about 180-200°c. Cut the pastry to size and line the pie maker or your moulds. Tear the lasagne sheet into pieces that will fit inside the pastry case, and then build the pies from the bottom up inside the pastry like so: a tablespoon of meat, some pasta, couple tablespoons of white sauce, sprinkle of parmesan, sprinkle of mozzarella and then repeat until the pies are full and ready for the lids to go on. Cook in the hot oven or pie maker until ready and then dig in.

# LOADED CURRY PIE

Not gonna lie, curry can be a ball ache to make, what with the base gravy and the time involved, not to mention the never-ending list of spices and family members not liking the same curries as each other. So I'm just giving you a quick and easy, mild, basic curry recipe here. You don't have to follow it; you can make your own or use any leftovers from ones you've made, use your favourite jarred sauce, whatever. The choice is yours.

## YOU NEED

2 small onion bhajis

4-5 tbsp your choice of rice (I use pilau for this)

1 chicken breast

¼ onion, finely diced

1 clove of garlic, minced or finely chopped

1 or 2 fresh chillies, finely chopped

¾ tin of chopped tomatoes

1 tsp each ground cinnamon, ground cumin, garam masala, ground turmeric, mild curry powder and ground coriander

Salt n pepper to taste

1 sheet of ready-rolled shortcrust pastry

Pie maker or moulds

## HOW YOU DO IT

Put the oven on and get the bhajis in to cook for 15-20 minutes until crispy. Prep your choice of rice, be it freshly made in a saucepan, microwaved, etc. and put to one side.

Dice the chicken into smallish pieces, then cook in a frying pan on a medium heat until done. Remove from the pan and put to one side. In the same pan, cook the onion for a few minutes until soft, then mix in the garlic and cook for another minute or 2.

Add the chillies, tinned tomatoes and all the spices, to the onion and garlic base. Mix and then let it simmer for a couple minutes while it reduces slightly.

Put the chicken back into the pan, stir into the sauce and then simmer for 5 more minutes on a low-medium heat. Season to taste.

In the meantime, get the pastry cut to size and put the bases in the pie maker or your moulds. Put a good tablespoon of rice in the bottom of the pies, then add a good amount of the curry, and finish by placing a bhaji on top. Cover with the pastry lids and cook until done.

# PHILLY CHEESESTEAK PIE

The good old American classic slapped into an English casing to give your tastebuds the best of both worlds.

## YOU NEED

¼ onion, finely chopped

¼ spring onion, diced

¼ red pepper, diced

160-180g steak, cut into small chunks

Salt n pepper

1 sheet of ready-rolled shortcrust pastry

Pie maker or moulds

## FOR THE CHEESE SAUCE

300ml double cream

Handful of grated red cheese

3 slices of burger cheese, ripped into chunks

1 slice of Applewood smoked cheese, ripped into chunks

## HOW YOU DO IT

Get a frying pan on a medium-hight heat. Chuck in both types of onion and the pepper, cook until soft, then put in a bowl to one side.

In the same pan, cook the steak until browned but not quite done, season with salt and pepper, then stir in the onion and pepper mix. Tip the whole lot back into the bowl and leave to rest.

## FOR THE CHEESE SAUCE

Grab a saucepan, stick it on a medium heat, add the cream and get it warm (not boiling or simmering). Add the cheeses, then stir until melted and the sauce is a good medium-thick consistency.

Now get the pastry cut to size for your pie maker or pie moulds and line them ready to be filled. Spoon the steak mix into the pastry cases and then pour over the cheese sauce until the pies are full. Top with the rest of the pastry to make lids and cook until done. Serve however you want.

# STEAK, BLACK PUDDING AND PEPPERCORN SAUCE PIE

If you like the three fillings, then you'll love this pie.

## YOU NEED

I sheet of ready-rolled shortcrust pastry

3-4 slices of black pudding

Knob of butter

I good-sized marbled steak (ideally ribeye or sirloin)

Salt n pepper to taste

I tbsp dried thyme or I sprig of fresh thyme

Pie maker or moulds

## FOR THE PEPPERCORN SAUCE

⅛ shallot, finely chopped (optional)

75ml brandy

160-170ml beef stock

110-115ml double cream

I tbsp crushed peppercorns

## HOW YOU DO IT

Get the pastry out the fridge and cut to size for the tops and bottoms of the pies, then line the pie maker or moulds. Fry off the black pudding in a big pan, then put to one side. On a high heat, add the butter and get the pan really hot, then cook the steak to medium or medium rare. Season with salt and pepper, add the fresh or dried thyme and baste with the butter until done. Take it out the pan and let it rest while you do the sauce.

## FOR THE PEPPERCORN SAUCE

Using the pan you cooked the steak in, chuck in the shallots and get them softish. Add the brandy and simmer for a minute or so until it reduces and the boozy smell goes. Make sure to scrape the bottom of the pan to mix in the meat juices. Add the stock and simmer again for a couple minutes until reduced by half. Turn the heat down, add the cream and let it thicken for a minute or so (do not let it boil) before adding the peppercorns and a bit of salt to taste. Take the sauce off the heat.

Cut the rested steak into smallish chunks and then add it to the peppercorn sauce with the black pudding. Mix it all together well. Spoon as much of the meat into the pastry cases as you can and then add as much sauce as possible to fill it up. Put the pastry lids on, then cook the pies until done and serve with whatever you want.

In my opinion, a good sauce takes
food up a few levels, whether it's from
a jar, straight out of a packet or
homemade. Here, I'm showing you some
stupidly easy sauces to make that
you'll need for some of the recipes in
this book. Don't worry, there's nothing
challenging in any of these.

Throughout the book, you can use shop-
bought alternatives if you want, but
some stuff you can't buy. So, you're
gonna have to get your spoons and bowls
dirty to make them. You'll also find
that with a lot of jarred sauces, you
need to add some seasoning etc. to get
the taste you desire. But hey, that's
the name of the game, right?

# SAUCY STUFF

# 4 CHEESE MAC N CHEESE

Who doesn't love a bit of mac n cheese? It's been a winner for years; you can add whatever you like and it still tastes banging.

## YOU NEED

3-4 rashers of streaky bacon (smoked or unsmoked)

500g macaroni

600ml double cream

2 good handfuls of grated Red Leicester

5 slices of burger cheese, ripped into bits

2 tbsp grated hard cheese (like parmesan)

Good handful of grated mozzarella

Pinch of paprika

2 chives, finely chopped

## HOW YOU DO IT

Set your oven to about 200°c or turn on your grill; whichever way you like to sizzle your bacon. Cook the rashers until crispy, chop it up finely and put to one side.

Get a saucepan, fill it with boiling water and put on a high heat to get it boiling. Add the macaroni and cook until soft and ready. It's always worth giving it a stir while cooking so that the pasta doesn't stick to the bottom of the pan.

In the meantime, get another saucepan and heat up the cream. You wanna get it hot, but not boiling or simmering. When the cream is hot (you can test it with your finger) add all the cheeses apart from the mozza, stirring to make sure they melt. Now keep stirring while adding in the mozza. You'll notice that it creates a really good cheese pull when lifting the spatula up through the sauce and that's what you want here. Add some paprika and mix it up.

When the pasta is ready, drain it and add to the cheese sauce. Stir it all in and make sure the cheese coats all the mac. Spoon it out into a serving dish or bowls. Sprinkle the bacon bits and chopped chives over the top and then dig in, getting that cheese pull as you spoon it out.

# CHILLI

You can use the same amount of cooked and shredded chicken instead of beef or pork mince.

## YOU NEED

Oil or cooking spray

½ onion, finely chopped

600g beef or pork mince

3 cloves of garlic, minced

1 tbsp tomato purée

1 tbsp ground cumin

1 tbsp ground coriander

1 tbsp chilli powder

½ tbsp ground cinnamon

Glug of red wine

1 tin of chopped tomatoes (or 1 carton of passata)

## HOW YOU DO IT

Put a bit of oil or cooking spray in a pan on a medium-high heat. When it's hot, add the onion and cook for a few minutes until it starts to soften. Add the mince and cook until browned (if using pre-cooked chicken, stir it in and then go straight to the next step).

Add the garlic, tomato purée, cumin, coriander, chilli powder and cinnamon to the meat. Stir to ensure it's all coated with the spices. Pour in the wine, then let it simmer and reduce before adding the tinned tomatoes or passata. Mix it up again and let it simmer for 5 minutes or so to start reducing the sauce.

Taste the chilli and then add more ground cumin, coriander, cinnamon or seasoning to taste if needed. Leave it to continue cooking slowly on a low heat while you prep whatever you're serving it with: rice, guac, tacos, nachos, tortillas, jacket spuds...

# BACONNAISE

## YOU NEED

2-3 rashers of streaky bacon (smoked or unsmoked)

5 tbsp mayo

2½ tsp Cajun seasoning

1½ tsp paprika

⅓ tsp salt

⅓ tsp pepper

⅓ tsp garlic powder

## HOW YOU DO IT

Get the bacon cooked and then chopped up into fine pieces. Start with the mayo in a bowl as your base. Throw in the rest of the ingredients, including the bacon bits, and stir everything together well. Leave it for 5 to 10 minutes for the flavours to start working. Taste and add more of anything you like to get the taste right for you.

# BLOODY MARY KETCHUP

Flavour your meal like you start your hungover morning, with hair of the dog.

## YOU NEED

200-250ml ketchup

¼ lemon, juiced

¾ - 1 tbsp Tabasco

1 tsp Worcestershire sauce

⅓ - ⅛ tsp horseradish

⅓ - ⅛ tsp celery salt

Pinch of paprika

Pinch of black pepper

Splash of vodka (optional)

## HOW YOU DO IT

Chuck it all in a bowl, mix together well and add more of whatever you want to get the taste right for you. Ideally, put the sauce in the fridge to chill for an hour or so but serve it up straightaway if you don't have the time.

# BURGER SAUCE

## YOU NEED

2 tbsp mayo

2 tbsp ketchup

½ tbsp American mustard (like French's)

Pinch of garlic powder

Pinch of onion powder

Pinch of paprika

## HOW YOU DO IT

Chuck it all in a bowl and mix together. It should taste pretty close to the Big Mac sauce. Just add a bit more of what you think it needs to get it right for your tastes.

# DIRTY SAUCE

## YOU NEED

3 tbsp garlic mayo (see below)

2 tbsp honey mustard sauce or dressing

1 tbsp buffalo sauce or hot sauce

## HOW YOU DO IT

Mix it all together in a bowl, then taste and add more of anything you think it needs.

# GARLIC AND HERB MAYO

## YOU NEED

5 tbsp mayo

¾ tbsp Greek yoghurt

2-3 tsp garlic granules or 2 cloves of garlic, minced

1 tsp dried mixed herbs

## HOW YOU DO IT

Put all the ingredients into a bowl and combine. Add more of anything to taste if you like.

# GUACAMOLE

## YOU NEED

2-3 ripe avocados

Good handful of coriander, finely chopped

2 good-sized tomatoes, finely chopped

¼ small red onion, finely chopped

1-2 chillies, finely chopped

1 clove of garlic, minced

1 lime, juiced

Salt n pepper to taste

## HOW YOU DO IT

Cut the avocados in half, remove the stone and scoop the insides into a bowl. Mash up with a spoon or fork. If you want the guac a bit chunkier then don't overdo the mashing. Add the rest of the ingredients, mix it up well and enjoy.

# GUINNESS CHEESE SAUCE

## YOU NEED

300ml double cream

Handful of grated Red Leicester

4 slices of burger cheese, torn up

Glug of Guinness to taste

## HOW YOU DO IT

Get a saucepan, pour in the cream and warm it up on a medium heat. You don't want the cream to boil. When it's hot enough (you can test by dipping your finger in) add the cheeses and stir so they all melt and the mixture turns a nice dark orangey-yellow colour.

Add the Guinness and keep stirring until the sauce is a good texture. You don't want it runny like water but not too thick either. The sauce should sit on top of your fries, or whatever you're putting it on, and not disappear into the food. Obviously, add the Guinness to your taste or use another ale; it's entirely up to you.

# KEBAB SHOP SLAW

## YOU NEED

1 large or 2 medium carrots, grated

1 medium onion, thinly sliced

⅛ white cabbage, thinly sliced

2-3 tbsp olive oil

1 tbsp lemon juice

Pinch of salt n pepper

## HOW YOU DO IT

Mix all the ingredients together in a bowl and then leave in the fridge for at least 30 minutes. Add more lemon juice, salt or pepper to taste as needed.


# CHIMICHURRI MAYO

## YOU NEED

125ml olive oil

125g fresh parsley, finely chopped (or 50/50 parsley and coriander, finely chopped)

4-5 cloves of garlic, finely chopped

3-4 chillies, finely chopped

4-5 tbsp red wine vinegar

1 tbsp dried oregano

Mayo to taste

## HOW YOU DO IT

Chuck everything except the mayo into a bowl and mix it all up real good. Leave the chimichurri for at least an hour to let all the flavours release into each other.

To make the chimichurri mayo, simply mix a tablespoon of the chimichurri with a load of mayo. Add more to get it right for your tastes.